RIGHTS NOT CHARITY

Protest Textiles and
Disability Activism

BY GILL CRAWSHAW

Common Threads Press

1	**FOREWORD**
3	**INTRODUCTION**
5	**TO BOLDLY GO...**
7	**RIGHTS NOT CHARITY**
9	**DISABLED PEOPLE AGAINST CUTS**
11	**JUSTICE NOT CHARITY**
13	**TRADE UNIONS**
15	**DISABILITY ARTS**
17	**THE ART OF PROTEST BANNERS**

21	**DWP DEATHS MAKE ME SICK**
23	**THE POOR LAW**
24	**NOT DEAD YET**
29	**BSL BRINGS US TOGETHER**
31	**NOTHING ABOUT US WITHOUT US**
33	**CONCLUSION**

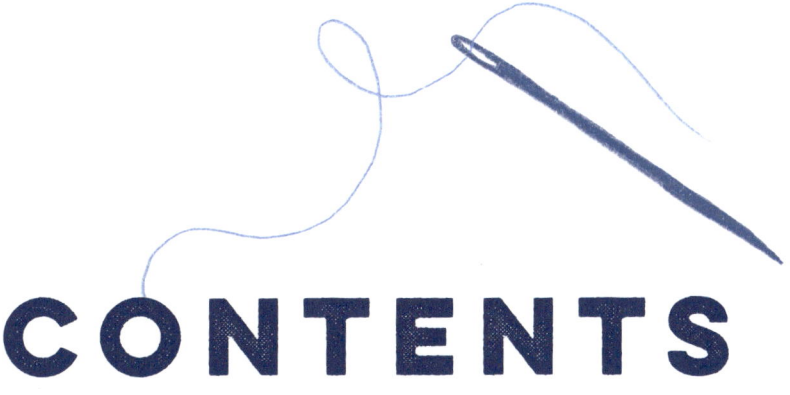

CONTENTS

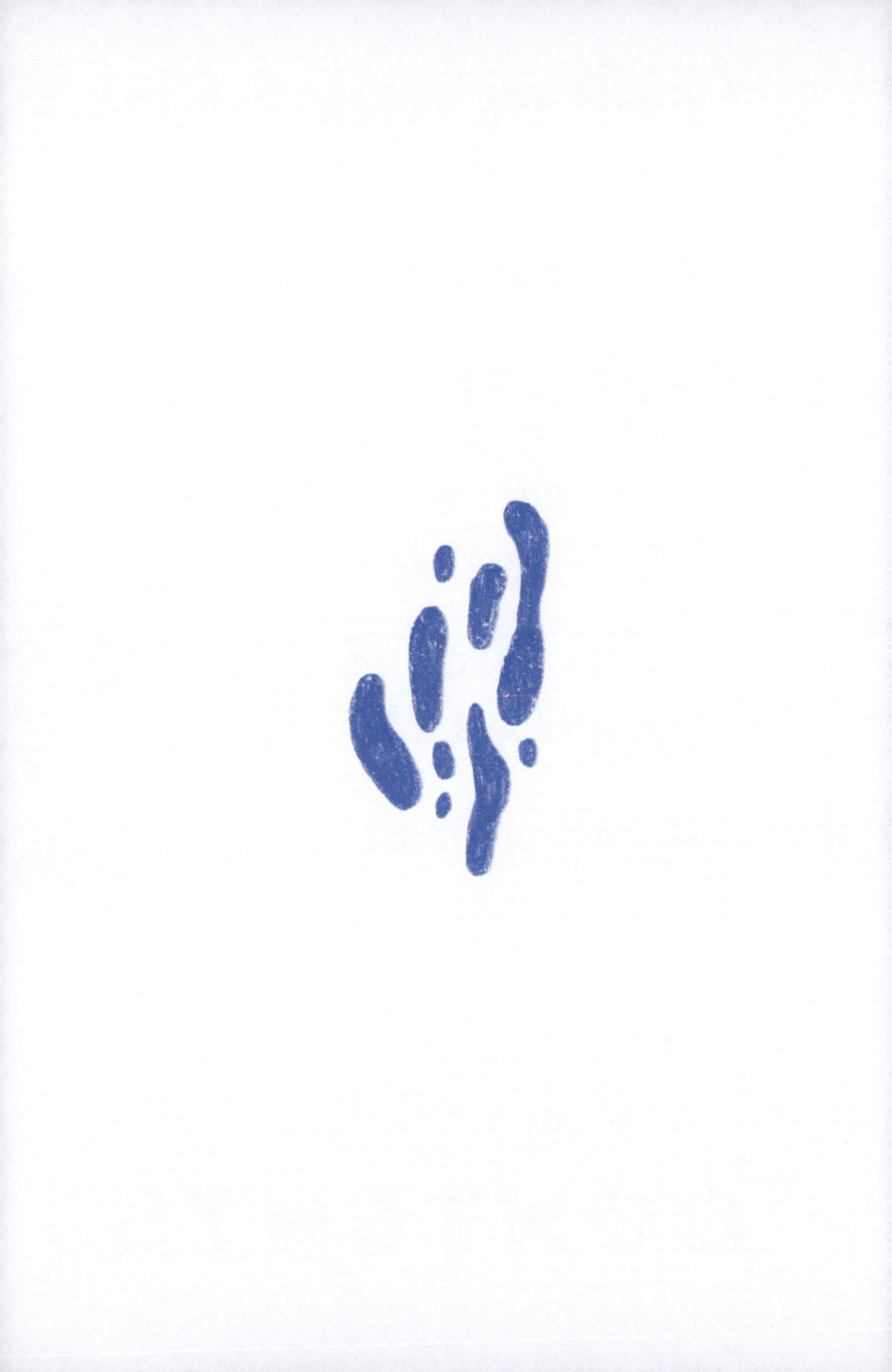

FOREWORD

Textiles and needlework have long been part of the fabric of disabled people's lives and history. From the workhouse and asylum through to occupational therapy in hospitals and day centres, needlework has been an activity intended to keep disabled people busy while being shut away from the rest of the world.

Institutional life for detainees in workhouses and asylums was harsh and highly regulated. Needlework, however, was encouraged, even compulsory. And institutions soon realised that they could profit from disabled people's work by selling the items they'd made.

Sewing, knitting and needlework remained core activities in hospitals, day centres, residential homes and schools for disabled people throughout the 20th century. As a form of rehabilitation, or in the absence of real jobs, disabled people were taught to knit, sew and weave.

Disabled activists and artists of today have embraced the radical possibilities of textile crafts at the same time as subverting their historical oppressive functions — to confound expectations and as a way to protest. They find textiles to be well suited for communicating challenging or confrontational ideas. They are drawn to textiles because they are versatile, portable and use materials and equipment that are affordable and close to hand.

In this context, the creation of fabric banners by disabled people and their organisations has a particular resonance. Disabled people are using textile materials and techniques for their own ends — as a call for rights and to support their collective movement. By doing this they are continuing the legacy of disabled needleworkers of the past, finding their voice and weaving a shared history of disability.

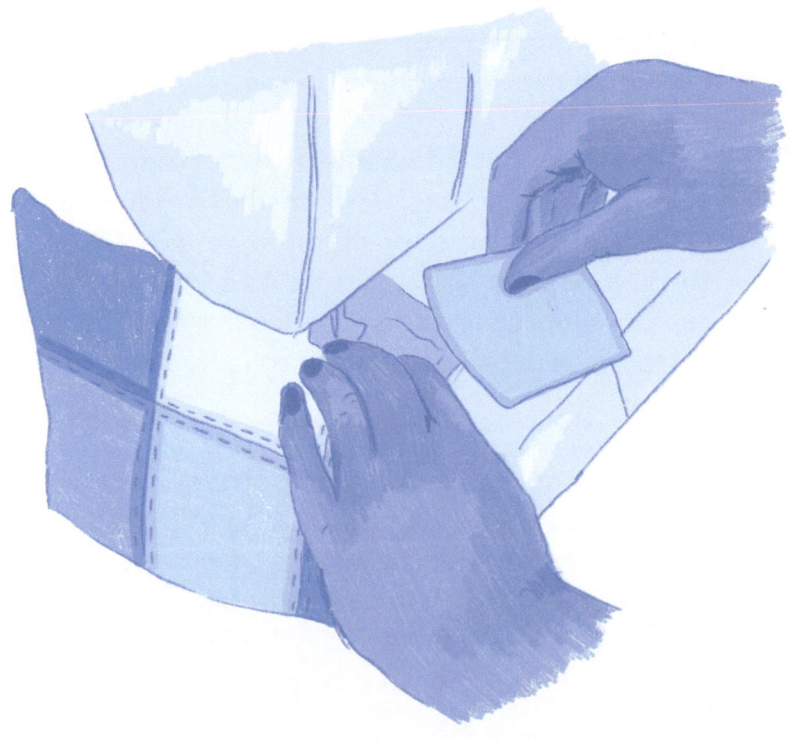

INTRODUCTION

The disabled people's movement in the UK has created some wonderful, attention-grabbing banners over the years, and this zine aims to bring some of them, and the campaigns they promoted, to a wider audience. It isn't a chronological or complete record; it loops back and forth, making connections across time.

In common with trade union banners, banners of the women's suffrage movement, and banners that are carried on demonstrations and rallies, disabled people's banners act as a form of protest or resistance — communicating messages about identity, pride, unity and justice. Whether quickly and roughly drawn or made with great care and skill, using repurposed materials or high quality fabric, they are a manifestation of the demands and aspirations of the disabled people's movement. While these have changed over time to meet new challenges, one particular slogan echoes down the years and appears on banners again and again: "Rights Not Charity."

These banners are evidence, and a reminder, that disabled people are organised, resilient, angry and strong. This is in stark contrast to the pervasive and damaging stereotypes of disabled people as dependent, needy and weak, perpetuated by disability charities and the welfare system.

Banners have amplified disabled people's call for fair and equal treatment, for dignity and justice, for rights not charity. Their messages are carried far and wide when they are captured in photos and film, then shared through press coverage and social media. Many of these banners are now lost, left behind or confiscated during protests, or lent out to other groups and movements. Even though they may be lost, they remain in people's memories as a source of great pride.

This zine is dedicated to all the activists who created, protested with and gathered under these and many other banners in the fight for disability rights and justice. And to the disabled activists of the future who will continue to protest and create banners to swell their voice — using textile materials and crafts, as well as virtual and online banners.

TO BOLDLY GO...

This story starts with a banner that has become legendary. It's one of the banners that accompanied the Disabled People's Direct Action Network (DAN) on many actions during the 1990s. Its witty slogan, "To boldly go where everyone else has gone before," was the backdrop for DAN's campaign for accessible public transport, when activists handcuffed themselves to buses and trains and stopped traffic for hours.

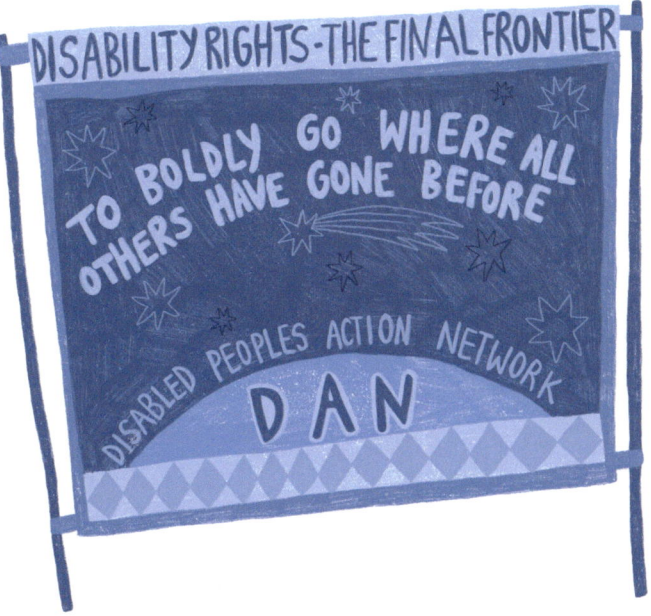

DAN was set up in 1993 specifically to take direct action, convinced that that's what the disabled people's movement in the UK needed at that time.

DAN had learnt from other liberation movements and had seen how effective direct action could be in pushing issues forward. For DAN, direct action meant non-violent civil disobedience. Members were prepared to break the law and to get arrested. While DAN actions didn't always end in arrests, they often did. The group's intention was to be confrontational and in-your-face.

Direct action is about taking your demand straight to your target. It's also about letting people know that you are angry and that things need to change. DAN's actions therefore took place in public. Having a bold banner in a striking design was part of the plan to be visible — to let people know who was protesting and why. DAN was often disruptive; the activists and their banner couldn't be ignored.

Perhaps aware of the power of a well-designed banner, the police confiscated this one at a DAN action. It was arrested, along with several activists! But unlike the activists, who were later released, the banner was never returned. An announcement in the DAN newsletter offered a pair of handcuffs as a reward for its safe return, but sadly it remains missing in action.

The bold pink and white design on a black background became the signature colours for DAN, also regularly reproduced on T-shirts as well as two other distinctive banners. Splashed across one of these others was a slogan at the heart of the disabled people's movement: Rights Not Charity.

RIGHTS
NOT CHARITY

In the 1980s and 90s, disabled people in the UK had become more vociferous as their demands for equal rights became more urgent. There was no law against disability discrimination until 1995, and the law that was passed had many flaws. Segregated institutions for disabled people, such as special schools, day centres, sheltered workshops and residential units, were still common. Disabled people were still excluded from much of community life, and they were impatient for change.

If disabled people appeared at all in the media, it was likely to be in adverts and television programmes that were raising money for charity. Disabled people were sick of being portrayed as tragic and needy in fundraising efforts for charities — organisations that were not even run by disabled people themselves.

In 1981, several organisations that were controlled by disabled people formed the British Council of Organisations of Disabled People (BCODP). BCODP provided a collective voice and created a strong foundation for the movement.

This was the background to huge demonstrations by disabled people in 1990 and 1992, outside ITV's Telethon, broadcast live from their London studios. Telethon was a 24-hour marathon full of celebrities and do-gooders, raising money for disabled people and other so-called 'worthy' causes. While those taking part were congratulating themselves on how selfless and generous they were, disabled people were fuming, accusing the show of being patronising in the extreme, even harmful in the way they represented disabled people.

The Telethon protests were a defining moment in the movement, a collective howl of rage and a flexing of power. DAN was formed the following year; ITV quietly dropped Telethon not long after.

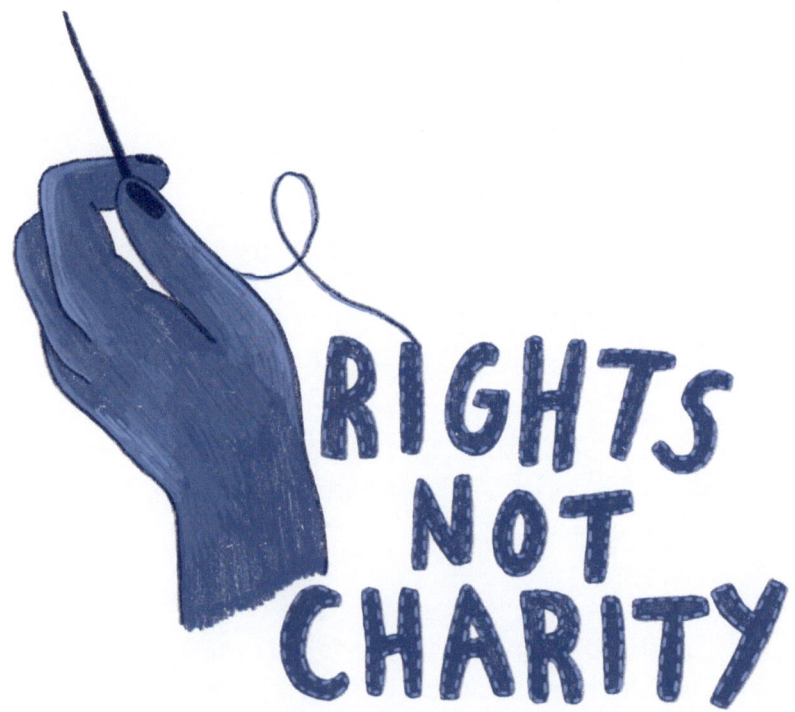

DISABLED PEOPLE AGAINST CUTS

Today, the slogan Rights Not Charity appears on the banners of Disabled People Against Cuts (DPAC), along with their circular logo of four clenched fists bursting out of a black triangle. DPAC is a disabled people-led campaign set up in 2010 to oppose the brutal impact of government cuts on disabled people and the poorest members of society. DPAC uses a range of methods to campaign including research, lobbying, online campaigns, direct actions and protests, and banners are always prominent.

Like other disabled activists before them, DPAC uses banners to articulate and publicise their wide-ranging demands. Sometimes a few demands are listed on the same banner, and have included calls to:

- Scrap work capability assessments
- Scrap the bedroom tax
- Stop the closure of the Independent Living Fund
- Drop the welfare reform bill
- Stop and scrap Universal Credit

In the current political climate, DPAC is a vital organisation, fighting the dismantling of the welfare state and speaking out against government austerity measures which target the poor while leaving the wealthy unscathed. They have groups around the country which welcome disabled people and non-disabled allies. Their contact details are at the end if you want to get involved.

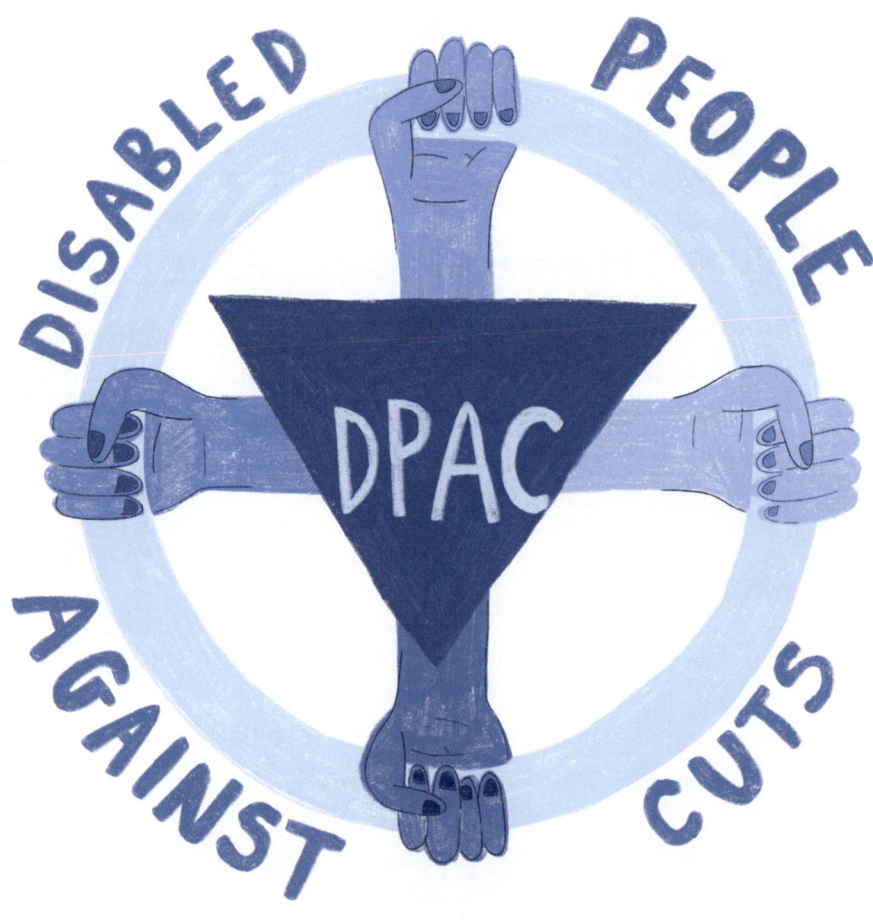

JUSTICE NOT CHARITY

"Not Charity But Social Justice" and "Justice Not Charity" appeared on banners carried by the National League of the Blind in 1920, demanding legislation to protect their rights and guarantee a minimum income for blind workers. Indeed, Justice Not Charity had become the organisation's motto because it summed up their ethos and purpose. In April that year, members of the league set off from Leeds, Manchester and Newport, marching 200 miles to London, gathering support for their cause along the way. The Birmingham Daily Gazette reported that:

> [...] they tramped along four abreast, bearing banners appealing for "Direct Government Support" and "No Charity," to the tunes of marching songs, the playing of bugles, and the shrill notes of the pipes of the various bands of ex-servicemen who accompanied them.

The purpose and determination of the people who took part in 'The Blind March,' walking for days with banners held high, is clear in a couple of surviving grainy black-and-white photographs. This determination led to the passing of the Blind Persons Act 1920, the first legislation in the world that specifically addressed disabled people's rights.

TRADE UNIONS

The National League of the Blind was registered as a trade union in 1899, but even before this, disabled workers were involved in trade unions. Many of them would have become disabled through the harsh and unsafe conditions of industrialisation in Britain, particularly in the country's leading industry: textile production.

Industrial injury was a feature of early textile factory work. As a result, there was a significant proportion of workers who had some sort of impairment. This wasn't necessarily associated with a lack of productivity, and many of these disabled workers continued or returned to work. They had little choice; they would have wanted to avoid the even harsher conditions of the workhouse if at all possible.

The conditions that workers faced led to early forms of disability activism. Dr David Turner writes on Swansea University's research into Disability and the Industrial Revolution:

> In August 1832, thousands of factory operatives carrying banners depicting deformed workers marched through Manchester calling for shorter hours in textile mills.

Many subsequent trade union banners emphasised the welfare support that unions provided for their sick or injured members. The pictures painted on the fabric depicted disabled and sick workers, conveying the message that disabled workers would not be abandoned or forgotten about by their comrades. The unions declared that they were "united to protect, not combined to injure."

Trade unions recognised the disabling effects of industry from the beginning, through bitter experience. They fought for better conditions with and for their disabled members, whether in work or not.

DISABILITY ARTS

Trade union banners are a prime example of how banners combine art and politics. This combination also defined the Disability Arts Movement, which emerged as the disabled people's movement became stronger and more confident towards the end of the 20th century. Many of the movement's banners are works of art produced by disabled artists.

Disability Arts evolved as the creative wing of the disabled people's movement in the UK in the 1980s and 90s. Defined as art by disabled artists that reflected the experience of being a disabled person, it was unashamedly political, rooted in the social model of disability*. The movement wanted to differentiate disability art from art that involved disabled people but was led by non-disabled artists, or from art by disabled people that didn't have disability as its subject matter.

Some people argued that any art made by a disabled artist was bound to reflect their experience of being disabled and living in a disabling society. Artists who worked in equal partnership with non-disabled artists felt that their approach wasn't reflected. Over the years, interpretations of disability arts have expanded and multiplied to become more inclusive and diverse.

Politics, particularly disability rights and justice,

remains at the core of disability arts today. It's no surprise that disabled artists are using their skills and creativity to make banners that are exhibited in art galleries when they're not being carried on demonstrations.

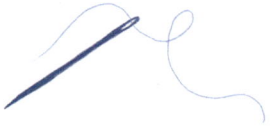

---

*   **The social model of disability:** This approach has been developed by disabled people. Their experiences have shown them that most of their problems are not caused by their impairments or by chronic illness, or because they are neurodivergent, but by the way that society is organised.

Disability is caused by barriers in society, where infrastructure, social organisation, and institutions have developed without taking account of people who have impairments, chronic illnesses or who are neurodivergent. These barriers disable people and prevent them from taking part in everyday life.

Disabling barriers include: prejudice and negative stereotypes, inaccessible buildings, inflexible ways of organising things (such as work), inaccessible information and communication, inaccessible transport, and fixed ideas about the way people should behave or look. The intersections of, for example, race, ethnicity, gender identity, sexual orientation and class impact on these barriers.

The social model dismisses the idea that disability is purely an individual problem that must be cured or pitied. Instead, the approach demonstrates that identifying and dismantling disabling barriers is a collective responsibility.

THE ART OF PROTEST BANNERS

In 2015, to celebrate 800 years of Magna Carta, Parliament commissioned nine artists, three of whom were disabled, to produce banners for Westminster Hall. Some of these banners reflect the artists' experiences as disabled people, and are relevant to the disabled people's movement.

Directly linking back to the 1830s and the beginnings of trade unionism in Britain, one of the banners created by Jason Wilsher-Mills was inspired by the Tolpuddle Martyrs. In 1834, this group of Dorset agricultural workers were severely punished for organising a union, sentenced to seven years deportation. While joining a trade union had recently become lawful, the Tolpuddle workers were arrested under an obscure law for swearing a secret oath. Following mass protests they were pardoned in 1836 and returned home a few years later. They became a popular cause in the early trade union movement.

Wilsher-Mills links their story directly to his own family history:

> I'm the son of a coal miner, so every summer my dad would take me to marches and I remember the banners, I have really strong memories of the coal miners' union

> banners... It was such a powerful story that I wanted to make a vivid image to go with it, that linked with those memories as a child of union banners.
>
> I wanted it to be hopeful, because out of that horrible thing that happened, the birth of the unions came about. People had a voice [...] for the first time.

These words echo the actions of those factory workers in Manchester, carrying a banner and demanding shorter hours. From the hazardous conditions of the mills and the resultant disabling accidents came collective action and safer workplaces.

Wilsher-Mills also created a banner commemorating the 1995 Disability Discrimination Act (DDA). This law was the culmination of decades of campaigning for anti-discrimination legislation in the UK, to protect disabled people's rights, and was certainly landmark legislation. Wilsher-Mills points out how the act made a difference to his life, being able to take part in leisure activities with his family — the sort of opportunities that others might take for granted.

However, the DDA was far from the conclusion that the movement had been hoping for. It was full of exclusions and couched in terms of 'reasonableness' that meant employers, education establishments and service providers could often get away with doing very little to end discrimination against disabled people. Many of them claimed that it would be too difficult and/or expensive to tackle the barriers within their own organisations.

Of course, protests continued — to improve the DDA or scrap it for something more comprehensive that was based on the social model of disability. The DDA is now subsumed into the Equality Act 2010. Meanwhile, the focus of protests has shifted to what have become more pressing issues: ending cuts to welfare and other public services, which are disproportionately affecting disabled people and even leading to deaths. DPAC is at the forefront of these protests.

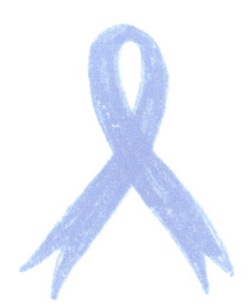

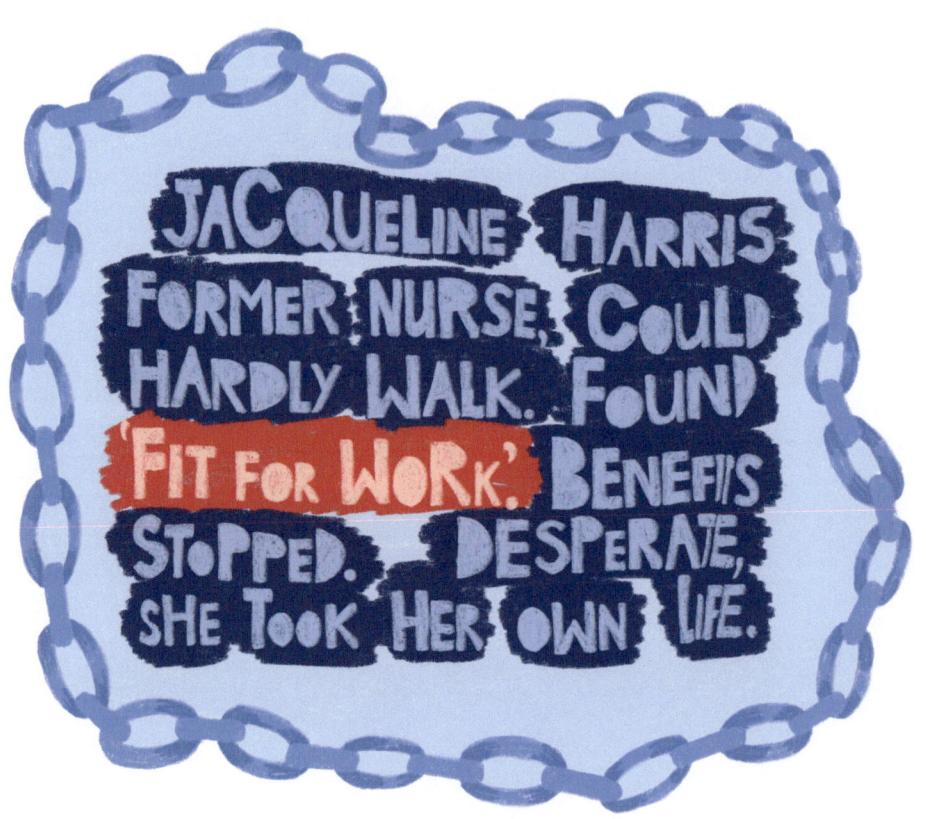

Illustration by Alice Bigsby-Bye.
Based on artwork by Vince Laws.

DWP DEATHS MAKE ME SICK

Artist and activist Vince Laws has been bringing attention to the shocking scale of the loss of life with his series of banners or 'shrouds' aptly titled *DWP Deaths Make Me Sick*. Stencilled and spray painted onto repurposed sheets, this ever-increasing collection of banners calls out the inhumane treatment of disabled claimants by the Department for Work and Pensions (DWP). They are a memorial to those who died after being wrongly assessed as being fit for work by the DWP. These decisions have led to many people's benefit payments being reduced or even stopped altogether, cutting off a vital lifeline and leading to extreme hardship, desperation and death — from stress, starvation or suicide.

Recent research by the Deaths by Welfare project shows that thousands of disabled people's deaths are linked to the DWP's failure to act, over decades, on numerous flaws in the benefits system. One piece of research, for example, connects just one area of the Conservative-Liberal Democrat coalition government's welfare reforms with an extra 590 suicides between 2010 and 2013.

Laws pay tribute to named individuals behind the statistics. He says of his shroud-banners:

They've been on street protests, in Parliament, and hung on gallery walls. They definitely attract attention. They're bold and vibrant, and when people read them they are shocked or sad or angry, or pleased to see their story represented.

In a similar vein, another powerful and moving banner that enacted both protest and remembrance is the one created by Gill Thompson and Maggie Zolobajluk listing the names of people who died due to benefit cuts and sanctions. 'Sanctions' are when the DWP stops or reduces someone's benefit for a period of time if they don't meet the conditions of their claim, even though there might be a good reason for this. Gill's brother was David Clapson, an ex-soldier who died penniless and hungry following sanctions.

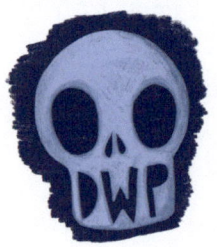

The banner was taken to the DWP headquarters in 2016, along with a petition signed by 31,000 people, demanding changes to the sanctions policy. Yet sanctions continue to be used widely and the DWP avoids taking responsibility for David's and others' deaths.

THE POOR LAW

In 1601, the Act for Relief of the Poor, known as the Poor Law, made it compulsory for parishes to collect taxes to support people who could not work. It was an early forerunner of the welfare state. It inspired one of the banners produced by Rachel Gadsden for the Parliamentary project.

Her banner pays respect to that law, but also to key figures and amendments that followed, including the founding of the NHS. "My narrative for the banner centres on my belief that society must be judged by its provision for those who are vulnerable," she explains.

Gadsden also makes a connection with her own experience as a disabled person:

> As someone who's lived with a really chronic lung condition all my life, and who relies on a huge amount of external support to keep me alive, I realised that I would probably have been one of those people that benefited from this actual Act.

NOT DEAD YET

Not Dead Yet UK (NDYUK) is part of a global alliance of disabled people, who oppose euthanasia and assisted suicide. NDYUK was set up in the face of growing campaigns aimed at legitimising the killing of terminally ill and disabled people, through the removal of legal barriers that protect against voluntary euthanasia and assisted suicide. NDYUK believes that individual disabled people's suicidal cries for help come from a lack of practical, emotional and medical support needed to live dignified lives, rather than from the 'suffering' they experience as a result of a medical condition.

The issue of assisted suicide is often a contentious subject. There are many disabled people who support and campaign for people's right to die, viewing this as a human rights issue. These campaigners call for dignity at the end of life, and dignity is also a primary concern for Not Dead Yet. Likewise, the call for appropriate assistance and support is a common factor across what is a complex and developing discussion.

NDYUK express this with the slogan, "We need support to live, not assistance to die," which also appears on a banner created by Brian Hilton and Wadiha Ahmed. While this may be a stark message, their banner depicts resilience and hope through a chain of disabled people, raising placards in protest.

Ahmed and Hilton made several colourful, bold banners for the movement, with Hilton designing and Ahmed stitching them by hand. The combination of modern design with traditional sewing techniques gives their banners an engaging aesthetic, while fulfilling the need for a banner to be clear and punchy. Their work includes a banner for the campaign to Save the Independent Living Fund, which helped people who needed high levels of support yet was closed by the government in 2015. They made banners for their local organisation of disabled people, Greater Manchester Coalition of Disabled People (GMCDP), as well as a banner for DPAC. Along with the familiar slogan "Rights Not Charity," the banner and its message are enhanced with an image of a megaphone, a familiar piece of equipment at DPAC actions.

Other disabled people's organisations who have made banners for marches and demos include the Mental Health Resistance Network, Black Triangle — the campaign galvanising opposition to the government's vicious attacks on disabled people's fundamental human rights — and WinVisible, a multi-racial community group of disabled women. The WinVisible banner has appeared at many London protests and pickets, on issues that are keenly felt by their members and other women: demanding a living wage for mothers; improving facilities and support for refugees and asylum seekers; preventing evictions; and, inevitably, benefits rights.

Disabled people have often made banners for protests and rallies quickly, working from home and using whatever materials are to hand: sheets, leftover paints and scraps of fabric. This doesn't make these banners any less effective, as these banners often rely on witty slogans and clear text. The Campaign for Accessible Transport, active in London from 1990-1993, stopped traffic and spanned the road with a painted banner that proclaimed, "At last! Disabled people catch the bus!", a slogan that DAN would use in later years.

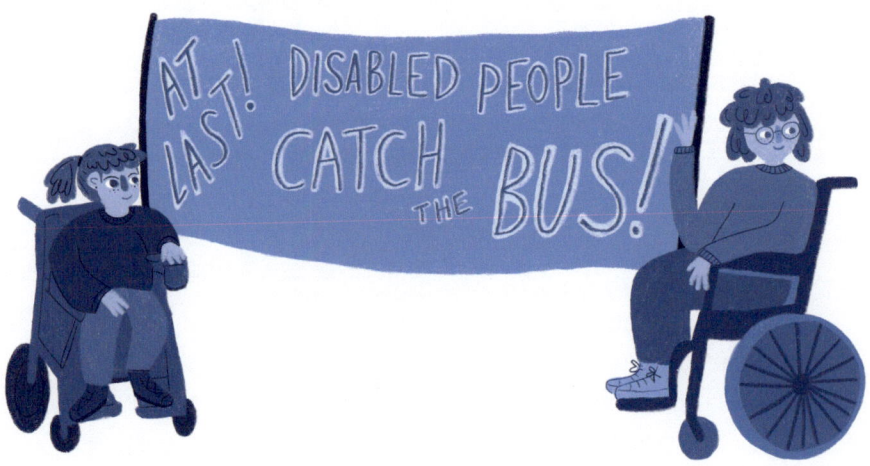

"Care homes are not real homes, Institutions are not solutions!" appeared on a banner in Leeds. It was created for a campaign against mistreatment of autistic people, sparked by abusive staff in a particular residential service run by a large charity, but its message is relevant to the wider demands for disabled people to be treated with dignity and respect, and for independent living.

The hashtag #FreeOurPeople at the bottom of this banner links it to the international disabled people's movement. This call for freedom, with its corresponding image of a disabled person breaking their arms free of the chains that bind them, is the rallying cry of the American activist organisation ADAPT (American Disabled for Attendant Programs Today).

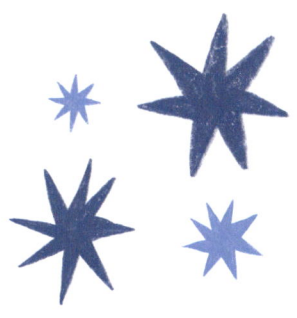

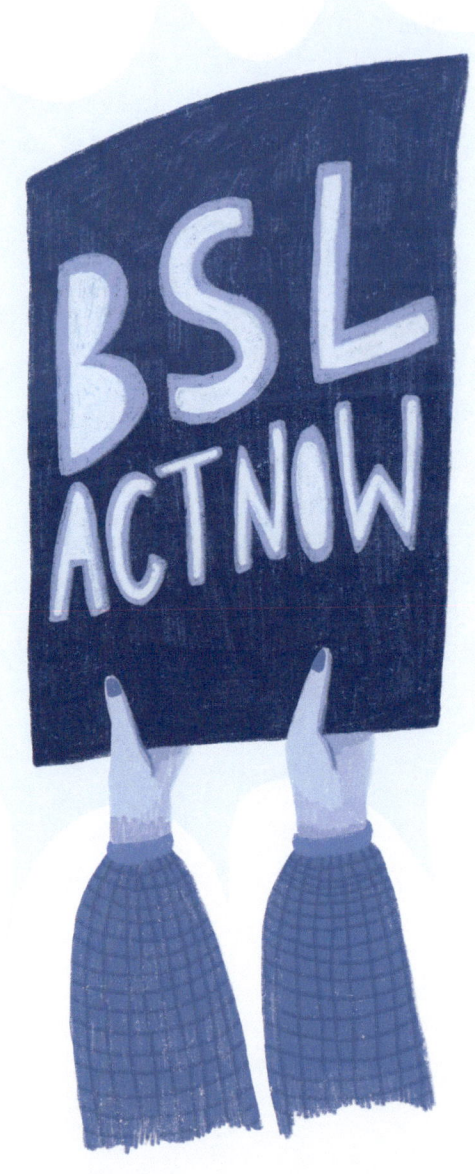

BSL BRINGS US TOGETHER

In 2022 thousands of Deaf people, along with hearing allies, attended a rally in Trafalgar Square, London. They were there to support the British Sign Language (BSL) Bill, which proposed that BSL should be given legal status. Banners and placards at the rally helped to raise awareness of the campaign, riding a wave of popular support for more widespread use of BSL and greater equality for BSL users. A home-made banner reading "BSL brings us together" celebrated this show of strength by the Deaf community. It also attests to language being a bridge across communities, in this case connecting Deaf and hearing people together.

The Bill passed through Parliament and became the BSL Act 2022. Campaigners hope that it will lead to greater recognition and promotion of the language. However, some Deaf activists, while cautiously welcoming the new law, have pointed out that it hasn't brought in any new rights for BSL users.

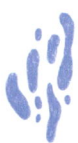

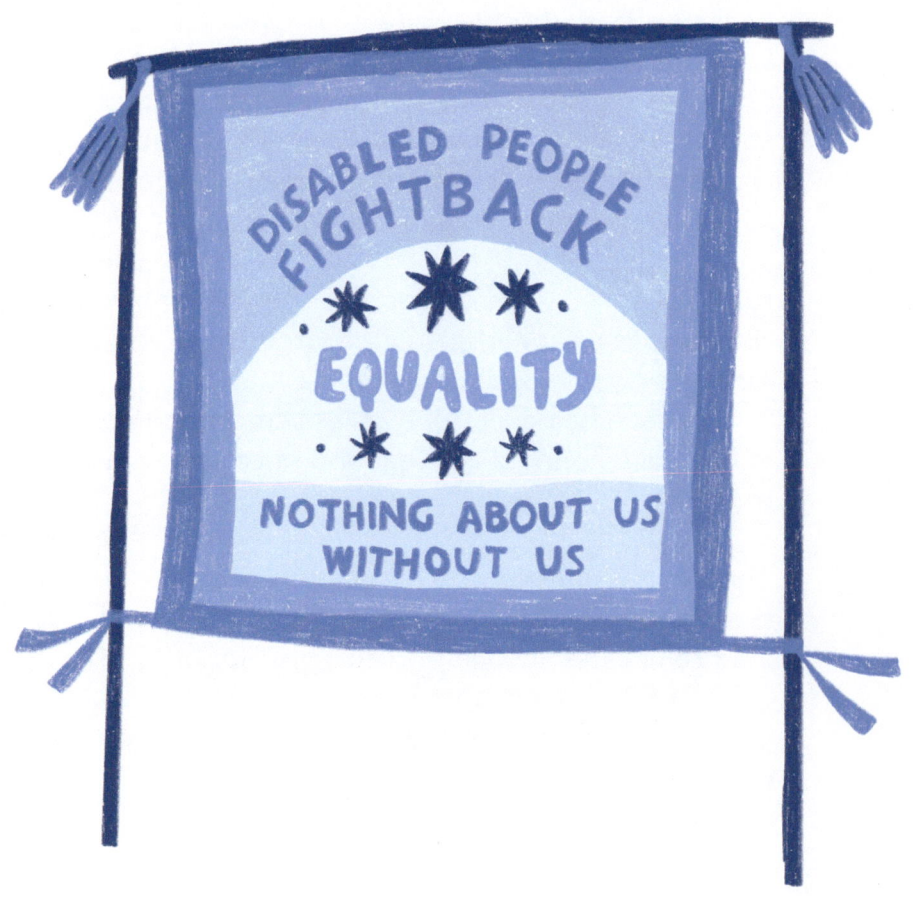

NOTHING ABOUT US WITHOUT US

During 2023, when this book was published, a landmark exhibition was running at the People's History Museum — the national museum of democracy — in Manchester. *Nothing About Us Without Us*, co-curated with disabled people, explored the history of disabled people's rights and activism.

Some of the banners mentioned in this zine were part of the exhibition. Another beautiful banner was at the centre of the display, brandishing the same slogan as the exhibition title: *Nothing About Us Without Us*. Along with Rights Not Charity, this is a bedrock of the disabled people's movement, advocating participation, self determination and empowerment.

The banner was made a few years before the exhibition, at a workshop for disabled people organised by the museum in partnership with a local community arts organisation. The group worked with Ed Hall, probably Britain's leading designer of trade union and other campaign banners. Artist Gemma Nash was in attendance, describing it as:

> A fantastic project [...] to design large-scale banners addressing issues of disability and

austerity. The project is a great way to give a voice to those most affected by the cuts to services and benefits that help Disabled and Deaf people to have independence.

This voice comes through loud and clear, with a montage of images and a series of slogans:

- Disabled people fight back
- Society makes people disabled
- Smash the barriers which exclude us
- End discrimination
- Powerlessness = pain
- No cuts to disability services
- Access to work

Like some of DPAC's banners, and certainly in the tradition of trade union banners, this *Nothing About Us Without Us* banner was designed to convey several messages together, and it does this brilliantly. This combination of ideas in one banner makes it versatile and timeless. It's in a museum at the moment, but it's bound to be carried through the streets again.

CONCLUSION

The disabled people's movement is not the only social or political movement to have created and displayed banners that convey their aims and demands. Indeed, in making their own banners, disabled people are carrying on the traditions of those who have gone before, as well as making connections with other struggles for liberation and justice.

Yet these banners are particularly important in disabled people's fight for justice. Disabled people have long been wresting control over the representation of their lives, needs and desires from charities and other organisations who claim to act on disabled people's behalf. And banners, with their powerful, witty, uncompromising messages, are another means of doing this. Banners allow disabled people to represent themselves in their own words, insisting that there should be "nothing about us without us."

One statement has endured since the early days of the movement. It has become a rallying cry that has been passed from generation to generation, as relevant today as it was one hundred years ago. Disabled people will therefore continue to stitch, pin, print and paint this demand onto their banners: **Rights Not Charity!**

JUSTICE NOT CHARITY

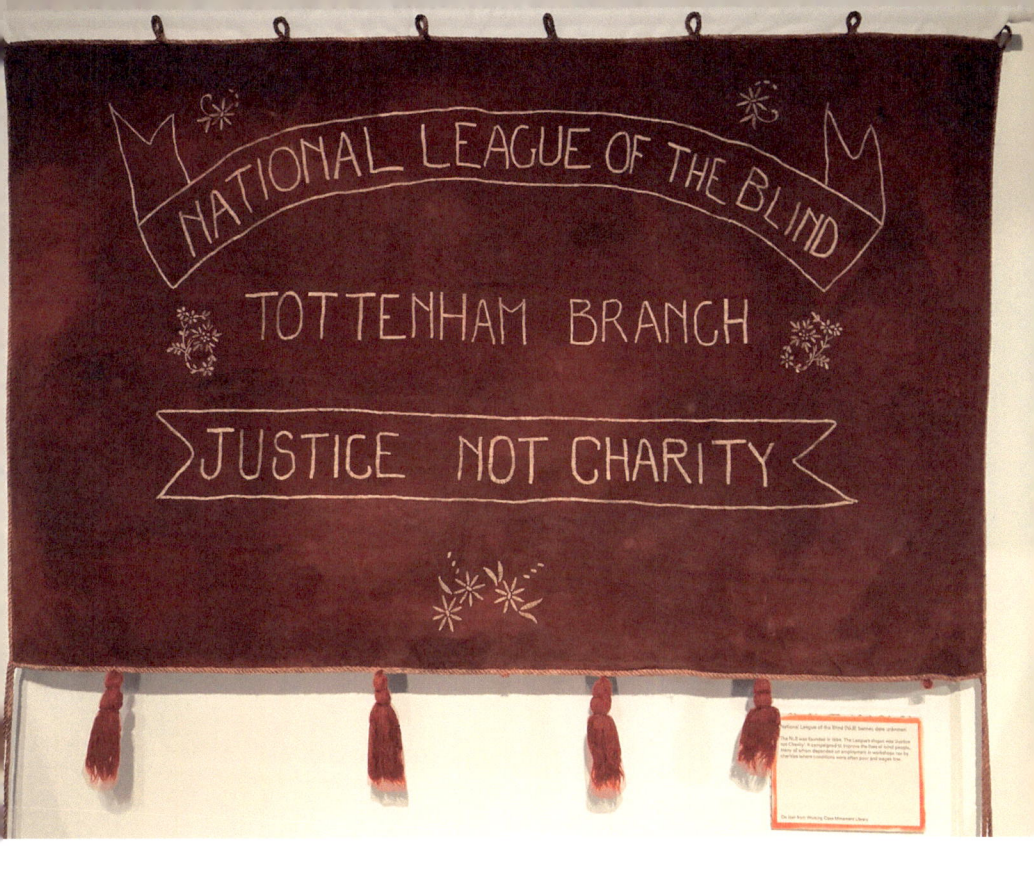

'JUSTICE NOT CHARITY' banner
National League of the Blind, Tottenham Branch
Collection of the Working Class Movement Library
Photo © Gill Crawshaw

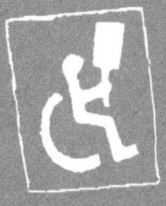

INCLUSION LONDON

GMCDP

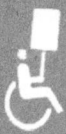

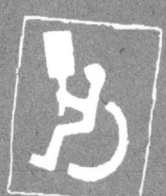

SAVE THE INDEPENDENT LIVING FUND

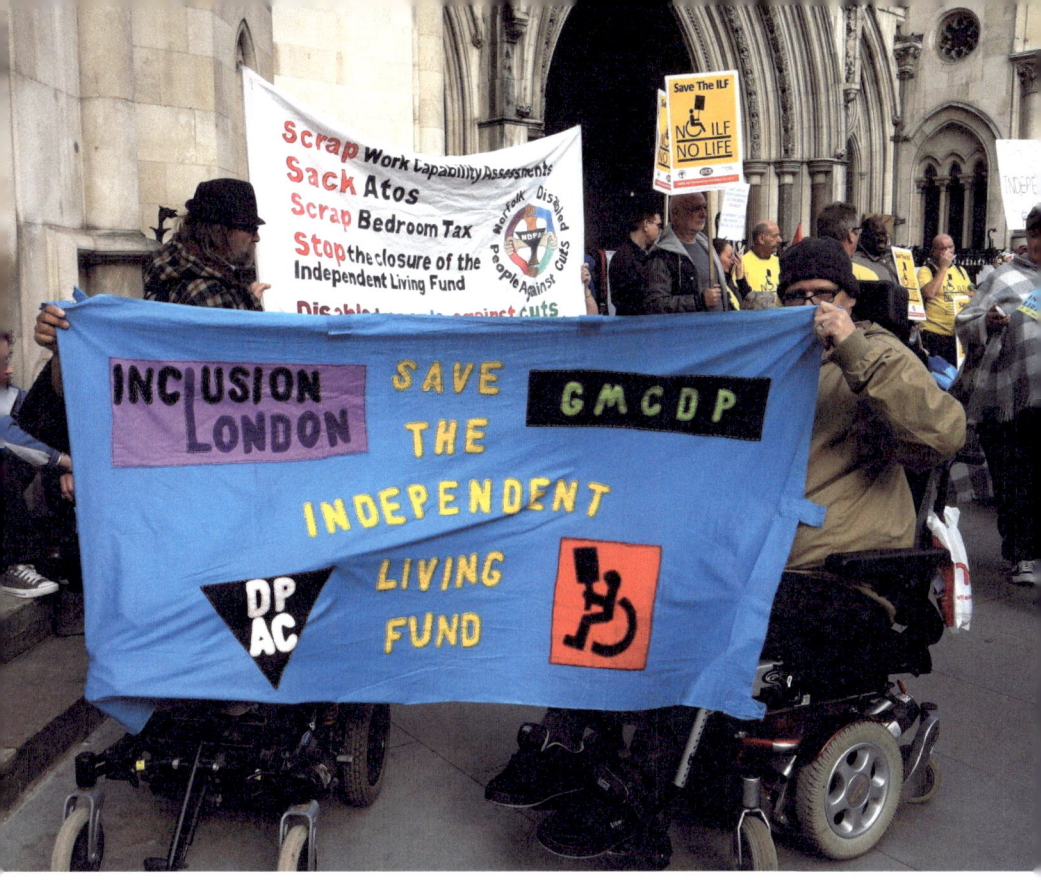

'SAVE THE INDEPENDENT LIVING FUND' banner
Wadiha Ahmed & Brian Hilton
Collection of the Disabled People's Archive
Photo © Brian Hilton

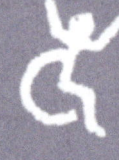

To boldly go where all others have gone before

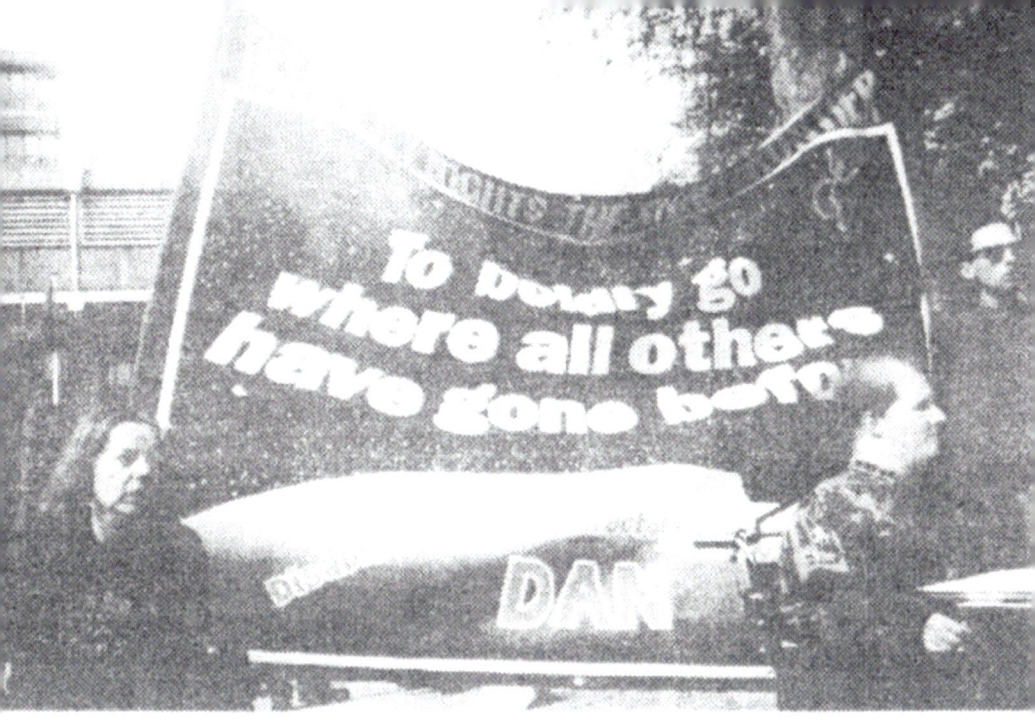

'DISABILITY RIGHTS THE FINAL FRONTIER' banner
Photocopied from the D.A.N. newsletter
© Disabled People's Direct Action Network

DISABLED
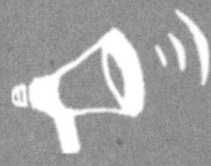

PEOPLE
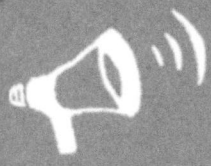

AGAINST
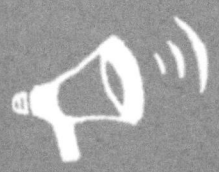

CUTS

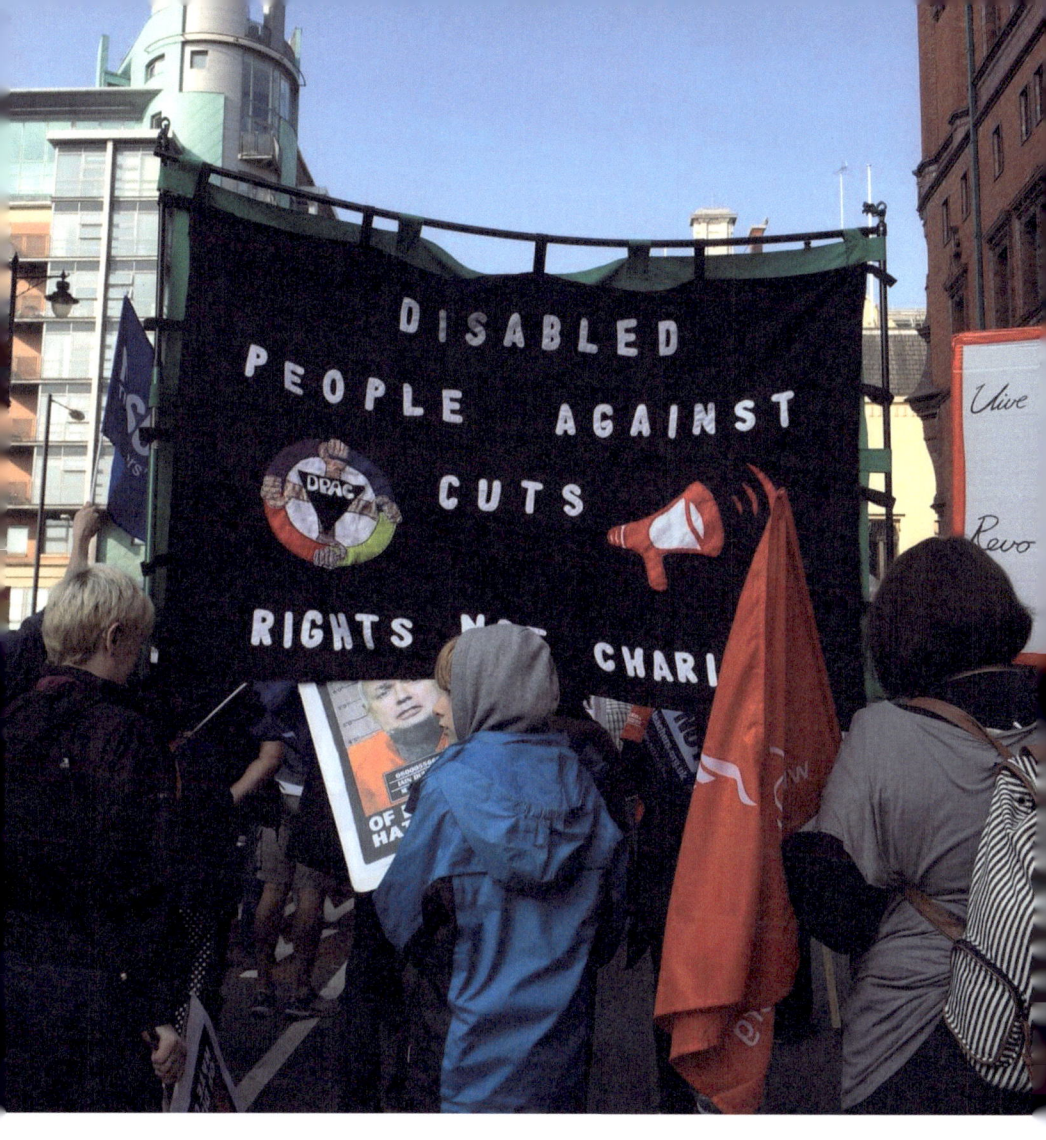

'DISABLED PEOPLE AGAINST CUTS' banner
Wadiha Ahmed & Brian Hilton
© Brian Hilton

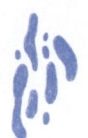

GMCDP Disabled People's Archive
www.disabledpeoplesarchive.com

Not Dead Yet
www.notdeadyet.org

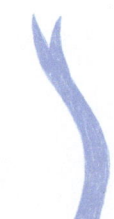

People's History Museum
www.phm.org.uk

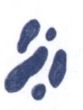

WinVisible
www.winvisibleblog.wordpress.com

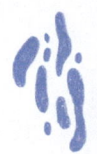

Working Class Movement Library
www.wcml.org.uk

FURTHER READING

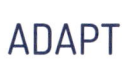

ADAPT
www.adapt.org

Black Triangle Campaign
www.blacktrianglecampaign.org

British Sign Language Act
www.bda.org.uk/bsl-act-now

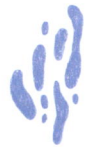
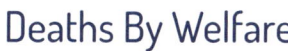

Deaths By Welfare
www.deathsbywelfare.org

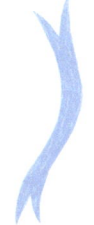

Disabled People Against Cuts (DPAC)
www.dpac.uk.net

Disabled People's Direct Action Network (DAN)
en.wikipedia.org/wiki/
Disabled_People's_Direct_Action_Network

DWP Deaths Make Me Sick
www.facebook.com/DWPDeaths

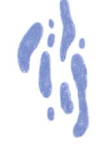

GILL CRAWSHAW is a curator who draws on her experience of disability activism to organise art exhibitions and events which highlight issues affecting disabled people.

Gill has curated exhibitions which have addressed representation of disabled artists (*Possible All Along*), charity (*Piss on Pity*), cuts to welfare and public spending (*Shoddy*) and access (*The Reality of Small Differences*).

Gill is interested in the intersection of disabled people's lives with textile heritage in the north of England, as well as with contemporary textile arts. In 2023, Gill organised an exhibition as part of LEEDS 2023, Year of Culture — *Any work that wanted doing* — where disabled artists were invited to respond to Gill's research into disabled people who worked in textile mills.

 ALICE BIGSBY-BYE is a disabled illustrator and textile designer based in Norwich, UK. They are an active member of the community and work on several projects including Queer Craft Club, Norwich Pride, Norwich Trans Pride, and the Norfolk Trans Joy Community Quilt. In addition to their community work, Alice is a passionate artist whose work often explores themes of disability, queerness, folklore, trans rights, and community. They are committed to using their art as a means of advocacy and representation, and to creating greater visibility and understanding of these important issues. You can find Alice on Instagram @DISGAYBLED.